TABLE OF CONTENTS

DISCLAIMER AND TERMS OF USE AGREEMENT:
Introduction
How It Works
   An Example (Where I Walk You Through)
You simply fill out the form to register:
You can have more than one adspace too!
If You Plan to Use Paid-Traffic
One of My Best Clever Extra Secrets!
Where You Can Get the "Cash" Code
I Have a Special Gift for My Readers
Meet the Author

Cash Code Pro
Let me Sell Ads on Your Website
©Copyright 2013 by Dr. Leland Benton

DISCLAIMER AND TERMS OF USE AGREEMENT:

(Please Read This Before Using This Book)

This information is for educational and informational purposes only. The content is not intended to be a substitute for any professional advice, diagnosis, or treatment.

The authors and publisher of this book and the accompanying materials have used their best efforts in preparing this book.

The authors and publisher make no representation or warranties with respect to the accuracy, applicability, fitness, or completeness of the contents of this book. The information contained in this book is strictly for educational purposes. Therefore, if you wish to apply ideas contained in this book, you are taking full responsibility for your actions.

The authors and publisher disclaim any warranties (express or implied), merchantability, or fitness for any particular purpose. The author and publisher shall in no event be held liable to any party for any direct, indirect, punitive, special, incidental or other consequential damages arising directly or indirectly from any use of this material, which is provided "as is", and without warranties. As always, the advice of a competent legal, tax, accounting, medical or other professional should be sought where applicable.

The authors and publisher do not warrant the performance, effectiveness or applicability of any sites listed or linked to in this book. All links are for information purposes only and are not warranted for content, accuracy or any other implied or explicit purpose. No part of this may be copied, or changed in any format, or used in any way other than what is outlined within this course under any circumstances. Violators will be prosecuted.

This book is © Copyrighted by ePubWealth.com

Introduction

Your AD Here!	Your AD Here!	Your AD Here!
Your AD Here!	Your AD Here!	Your AD Here!

This technique I am about to show you is nothing new on the net; however with that said, the way I show you to use it is rather unique.

It is used by some very large companies like Alexa and it never fails to bring in money quickly.

There are many variations of this technique and I have heard it called "The Magic Code," The Magic Money Siphon" and tons of other hype and BS but it is nothing difficult or magic; it is good clean legal marketing skill!!!

Like everything I teach always Test, Tweak and Test Again!!!!

I think you will be extremely amazed at how simple this technique really is but don't be fooled; most of the profitable marketing techniques on the internet are simple and rather easy to implement.

It will take about 10-days to really master this technique and I will give you all the information and websites necessary to put it into action swiftly.

Oh, once you mater this technique, you will be using it in everything you do online.

This is because you will have discovered a very quick, convenient and easy way to add as many additional income streams as you want and make therefore as much money as you want.

How It Works

This technique allows you to add just 1 simple string of code to any webpage you have, and immediately you start to see some big money start rolling in.

One variation of my system is now being used by **Alexa.com**: http://alexa.com/.

Alexa has a block of **button banners** at RIGHT on most of their pages that other advertisers spend quite a lot of money for.

Every single minute of every single day, 365 days a year, massive numbers of people are visiting these pages and clicking on these ads.

And each time they do, Alexa gets paid.

Alexa does nothing but add this special "cash" code to their webpages, and then the money automatically rolls in.

Alexa does NOT have to manage anything really; other than perhaps just making sure their webpages remain working with little or no downtime.

The trick of course lays more in just getting traffic to your site – and there are a number of ways to accomplish this successfully; and which will be discussed more at length in the following pages.

But for now I want you to just better familiarize yourself with this technique, and imagine how it can start working for you.

See just below an example of Alexa selling off ad spaces on their Home Page…

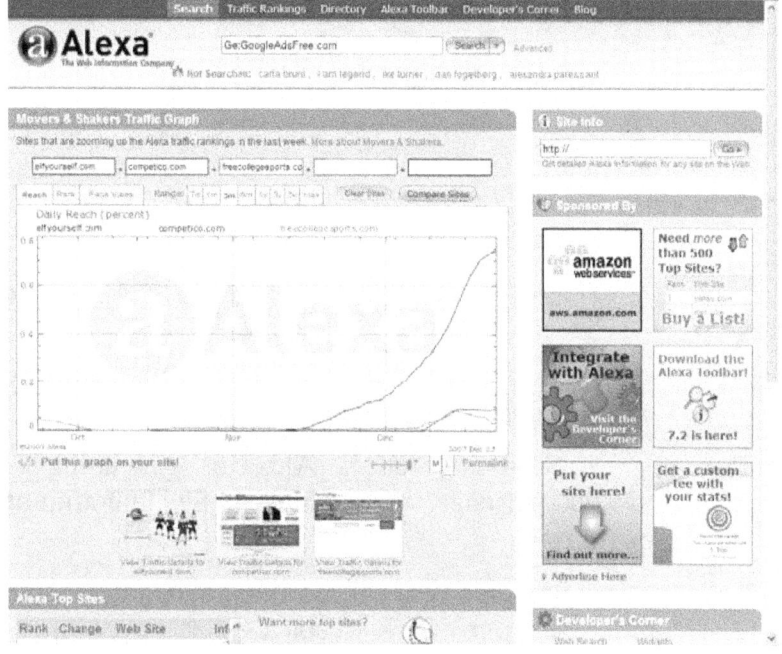

Would Alexa do this if it wasn't working greatly for them?

Alexa is run and operated by some pretty sharp people – so I'd see the wisdom in their example if I were you! If you click the tiny little link that says "**Advertise Here**" it will take you to the pricing page. On that page you will see the following prices:

Sponsored Listings

Alexa offers placement of up to 6 sponsored listings on the front page of Alexa above receive up to 1 million page views per day and offer the most visible branding opportu

- Ads are 125 X 125 pixels
- No flashing or animated ads
- Ads are linked to the URL of your choice

Pricing for each of the 6 sponsored listings begins at $15,000 per month, which trans affordable rate at approximately $.50 CPM. To inquire about sponsored listings pleas

Notice it says that just these little button banners cost **$15,000** per month?

So the revenues Alexa is generating is 6 x $15,000 per page, which comes to **$90,000 a month <u>per page</u>!**

Imagine yourself receiving $90,000 a month quite passively from YOUR webpages.

And the best part is: **Someone else sells off your ad spots for you!**

The online companies offering you their "cash" codes handle everything for you!

You merely focus on putting up pages, getting traffic, and adding their codes.

They then take everything from there, and pay you for allowing THEM to share <u>YOUR</u> pages!

You can then expand on this and take this as large as you want to go.

There are a good number of online companies that offer what I refer to as "cash" code.

These *strings of code* can be generated instantly

8

when you set up an account *(usually free!)* and go to their section that allows you to set the "parameters" for the code you get at the end.

"Parameters" just means things like:

• Your Ad *Type* (e.g., text banner, etc)

• Whether Horizontal or Vertical *Layout*

• *Size*

• Background *Color*

• Headline *Color*

• Description *Color*

• Etc.

After you set these parameters and compose your ad *(if textual)* or upload you ad *(if a banner)* you can then set your ad's cost and for what *duration*.

This is the truly fun part because this step is where YOU decide *(**not** someone like Google!)* how much you are going to charge when someone places and ad on your page.

You will want to be fair as if you charge too much, the advertiser may not make his money back sufficiently – and he may decide not to renew his ad each term. You can set your *duration* for:

• 1 day

• 7 days

• Or 30 days if you choose

After setting your *duration*, you can then "click" to generate your code!

From here, you simply add that code at some location on your webpage or webpages.

An Example (Where I Walk You Through)

You can sign-up for FREE with many of the Ad Sell-Off Services* available online *(*I will provide you a good list shortly)*. A great one – and my favorite - is http://www.Etology.com

When you arrive at Etology all you have to do is sign-up by clicking **SELL ADS** in the upper menu bar.

Then you can register your site and start building your adspace "cash" code, and start automatically selling off ads right away, and watch the money rolling in! It takes just seconds to enroll and get started.

You simply fill out the form to register:

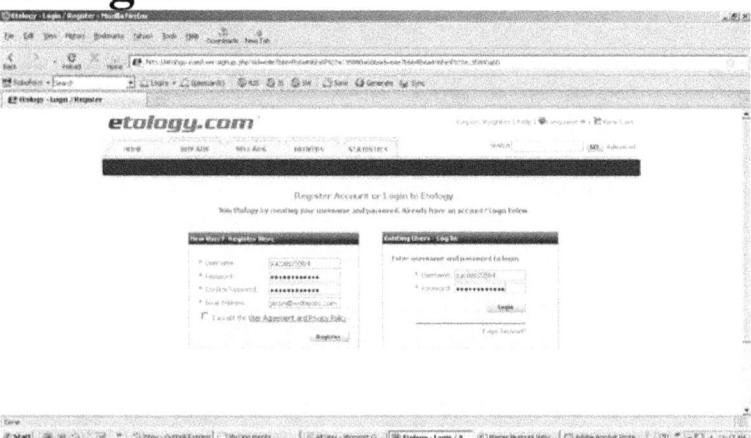

I'm telling you nothing could be easier! These companies want you to be successful because they get a commission of every ad they move on your behalf. Therefore, they make all this from start to finish easy as heck! Most people think there must be some catch – and the ONLY catch is that these companies stand to share a little in YOUR success. So of course they make it very, very easy. Just don't make the incorrect assumption that because this is very easy it couldn't possibly work *(if you do you'll miss out on all the Fun and MONEY!)* Once your account is set up, simply begin by creating an *adspace*:

Once your website is registered proceed to the next step of building your ad.

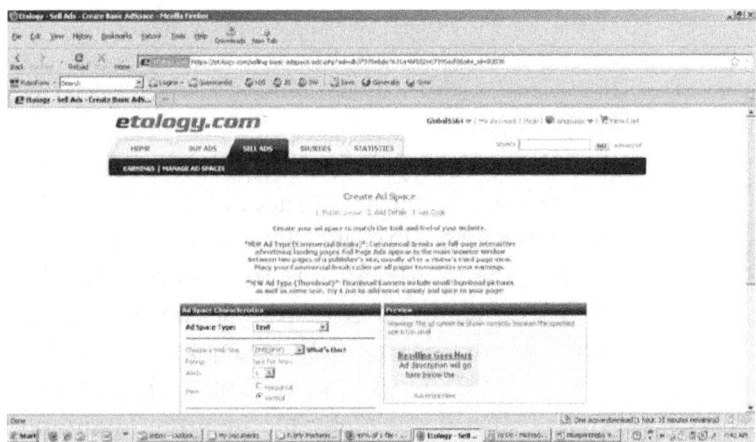

This feature allows you to control what someone sees on your specific page in terms of ad space **size**, **shape**, and **colors**, etc.

Also, here you determine the **number of ads that appear** in your *adspace* as well as if your ad(s) is a **banner, text, thumbnail** or **other**.

People will be filling these spots when they advertise on your page. There will naturally be a small link somewhere on the resulting page that reads: **Advertise Here** Don't concern yourself with thinking that *YOU* will be the one selling off these spaces – YOU WON'T! That's what companies like *Etology*™ do on your behalf.

Once you set up your account, set your parameters, and then create a code(s), these companies automatically provide you a page in their catalog so that your site visitors can click and visit this page and buy your spots. That's an extra exciting additional bonus when using these "cash" code providers! You of course can even promote separately if you wish to "speed things up" simply by advertising your cataloged webpage with them – but this is entirely your choice.

The catalog allows people searching these companies to easily find you based on such things as tags, relevant content, etc.

So it's very easy to get advertisers on your page. Regardless, once a number of advertisers secure an ad each on your page(s), if you are priced reasonably and where they can profit easily they obviously will renew.

Firms such as Etology often have an automatic renewal notice emailed to your advertisers letting them know when to pay again; or autopay in case they don't want to fool with manually doing so.

Once you've outlined your adspace's *parameters* you'll decide how much to charge someone to advertise on your specific page or pages.

Create AdSpace

1. Build Layout 2. Add Details 3. Get Code

Set the pricing and description of your adspace. We have added some recommended pricing for you but you should change it based on the expected traffic of the space. You can always edit this information through our system.

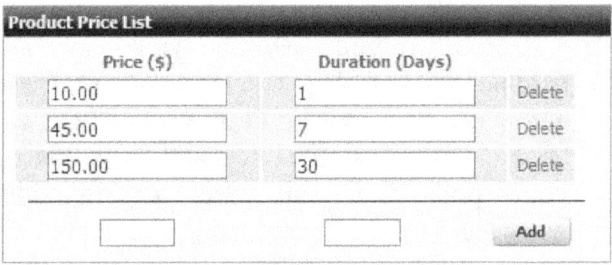

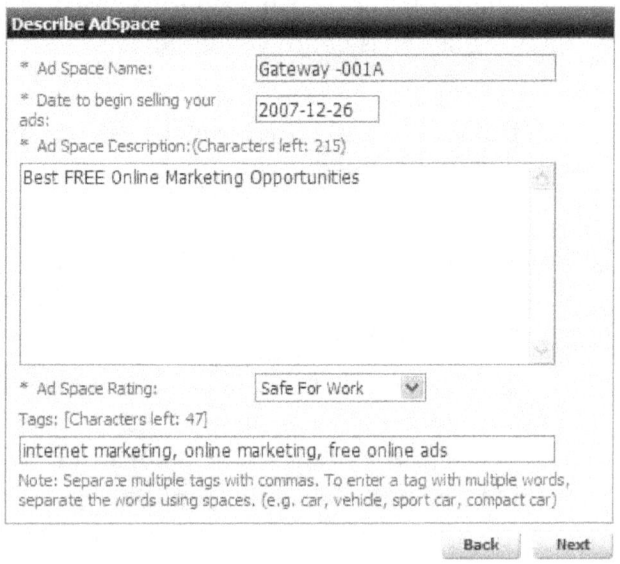

This is where you carefully determine exactly how much to charge.

If your web pages are getting traffic without you having to spend money, then you can go as low as you wish as you stand to gain regardless.

You can accomplish this type of traffic a variety of ways including *(but not limited to)*:

• Search Engine Optimization Tactics (SEO)

• Viral Drivers (such as ShareThis.com or tell-a-friend scripts)

• Link Exchanges

• Articles you post free

• Free Classified Ad Sites

But you may equally want to direct paid-advertising traffic to your webpages, and then offset your ad costs using this same system.

Say for instance that you are spending **$900 a month** at Google on PPCs and this allows you to occupy the **TOP positions** in every single keyword you use.

Further, assume that you allow just 6 *adspace* to be filled on any one webpage you have. Dividing $900/month by 6 equals just $150/month to any advertiser running their ad on your landing page.

Selling off all 6 spots *(which is EASY!)* guarantees

you eliminate your ad costs *(and your main offer rides for FREE!)*.

And again, this can always be used to offset your ad costs.

IMPORTANT! When directing traffic from Google to your webpage, you should avoid adding the cash code on the page where visitors arrive as Google tends to punish your rank a little.

In order to get around a potential "slap" by Google or any other search engine, simply create a doorway page first (more on this later), and from there have a link that people click to your main page containing the cash code and adspaces.

After you've set up your tags *(these allow the right people to be able to advertise on your adspace)* and everything else, you will want to get the *cash code* and edit it into your select webpage:

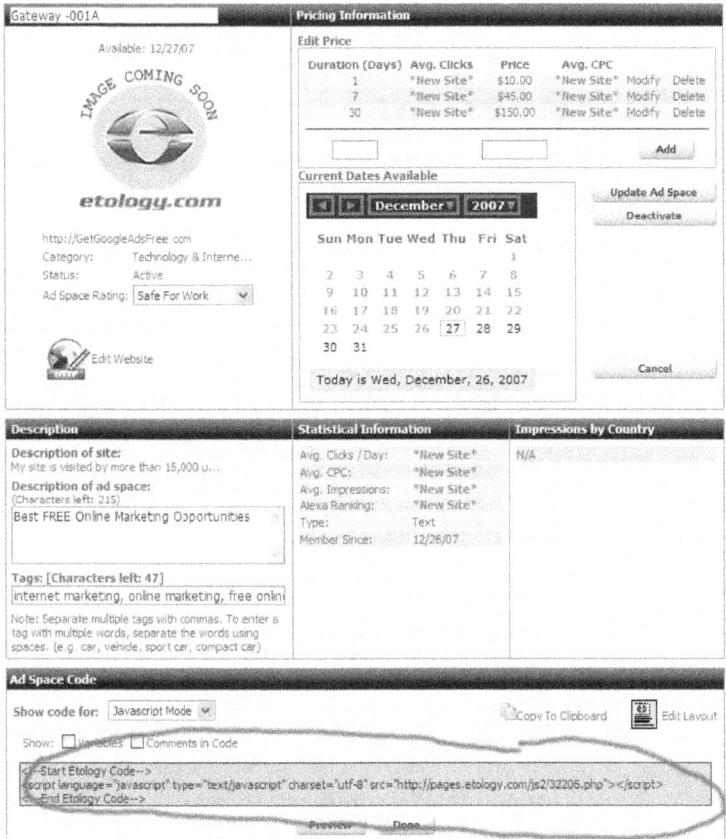

Again, nothing could be easier!

You can then see at a glance inside *your account* all the statistics concerning your adspaces and them selling off ad space to others! …

You can have more than one adspace too!

Using *multiple adspaces* you can add more than one patch of code to a website, and therefore <u>sell off even more spaces if and when needed</u>!

You just add the code whenever and wherever necessary in order to offset your PPCs costs if you choose to direct paid-advertising traffic to your webpages!

Whether free traffic or paid traffic, it doesn't change the fact that you can force any webpage you have, create or upload to the Web into an instant money-generating machine.

If You Plan to Use Paid-Traffic

Mostly I like to create webpages that will just get picked up and heavily indexed by search engines and thus result in free traffic.

Additionally, I take advantage of many free traffic generating techniques readily available online; and then have that free traffic directed to my webpages that also contain my *cash code*.

This way I truly create free moneymaking machines that are like little robots that crank out real money for me all day long, and even while I sleep.

You can of course imagine the fun this creates for me, as I sort of feel like I have the best-kept secret in town *(or in the world for that matter!)*

But I've equally used this same exact system when using paid-traffic very successfully as well.

The chief difference is that when doing so I try to deliberately offset my ad costs by using this cash code to sell off enough spaces at the prices I select in order to exactly nullify all most costs completely; and which allows me to run a particular offer as a sort of *"free-ride-along!"*

You can do this too if using any form of paid advertising.

Say that you now have your account set up with something like *Etology*, you would now have a page that people could be directed to if and when they come across your page online **(such as after having either clicked to your gateway or landing page from your PPC ad at Google).**

You'd simply do two things:

1. Set up a doorway page first (so Google or any other search engines don't slap down your ranks when using their paid advertising services; such as AdWords)

2. Carefully figure how much you'll be spending on this form of advertising to get traffic, and then divide it by the number of spaces you intend to sell off; and so that once purchased by others your advertising becomes free through offsetting, and being paid for by other advertisers.

People will be drawn to your pages and the opportunity to by ads simply because it puts them before the same size audience, but for a mere fraction of the costs.

One of My Best Clever Extra Secrets!

You can take my system here as high as you want to go! One of the BEST ways is through paid-traffic so that all your offers receive highly-targeted visitors.

The only real concern, however, is the costs involved for producing such large volumes to begin with; assuming of course you don't already have lots of free traffic coming to your site's pages.

But rather than try and convince you of just how big you can take my system, let's concentrate on the topic of *pre-capitalization* (which I call *"precapping"*)

Since *CashCodePro* promises to generate money from your webpages, and which require traffic to be flowing to those pages and which often has to be purchased, some people don't want to even risk any upfront moneys to "jumpstart" the system.

They understand that after their traffic-generating ads are running people will inevitably start buying enough ads to soon eliminate their own costs – but they are a tad shy about spending any money to get started (and if so, they may end up missing out on what could have been a really great opportunity to earn more money from the Web than they even thought possible!)

So I want to point this out in case you ever start thinking my system isn't for you. Anyhow, let's start off by assuming you haven't even started running any PPCs yet, although you may have already designed and built a nice landing page advertisers can buy space on.

Helpful Tip: If Google lowers your page quality score, as already instructed, create a gateway page first and have your PPC ads direct there, and when people arrive there and click further it takes them to the actual landing page that advertisers will share with you.

But the thing is you DON'T have to be advertising at Google or anywhere else to now have this sell-off page at Etology!

You could do no advertising at all and just let your Etology page sit there.

But this is where precapping comes in! You could just as easily visit a number of Forums and ask other members if they'd be interested in advertising on your site.

You could also post a banner that redirects to your *Etology* sell-off page, and place it at something like the **Free Advertising Blog:** http://www.free-advertising-blog.com/.

Or you could post an announcement here at the **Free Ad Forum:** http://www.thefreeadforum.com letting people know what you intend to do, or just have your notice go directly to your Etology sell-off page!

People nowadays more than ever want to get some great quality targeted-advertising, but for a nice discount.

Your ability to provide a venue for which they may do so, proves as a very, very valuable service and benefit to them.

Letting them know in Forums and in Blogs is perfectly within the etiquette of online users, and will actually be welcomed.

Remember: You are making the same exposure before Google's audience for them, but at a fraction of the costs *(often being just 10% of what THEY would be forced to pay otherwise if they ran PPCs directly!)*

Here's how to word your ad/announcement …

"Hey everyone! You can get 90% OFF the usual AdWords costs with this!"

…and then place a hotlink behind where it reads '**with this!**'

Or, if you'd rather do so and be less blatant, just

write in some Forums and happen to mention what you have and a convenient link to your Etology page (or whatever free ad sell-off service you end up using).

But there is a more direct way to start getting advertisers, but it costs just a little money ...

You can actually use the very thing you are trying to offset your ads with: **AdWords!** Here's a very clever ad I've used now and then for some immediate, instant, highly-targeted results which gave me all the advertisers and "jumpstart" I needed:

Textual version:

90% OFF Goooogle PPCs
Accepting Just 10 Advertisers Now
or in the Next 24-hrs -- Hurry!
YourLandingPageHere.com

Screenshot:

90% OFF Goooogle PPCs
Accepting Just 10 Advertisers Now
or in the Next 24-hrs -- Hurry!
YourLandingPageHere.com

It's important that you deliberately misspell 'Google' using at least four *o*'s as to use 3 or 4 they won't allow you to set up an AdWords ad *(at least without requesting an exception)*; but people will know what you mean.

You can then do one of two (2) things here:

1. You can simply direct ALL incoming traffic to your Etology-like sell-off page

2. Or, you can direct leads to a lead-capture page so that you can reuse those leads over and over again **(I prefer this one!)**

The reason you'll most likely want to choose the

second option above is because the first means someone just happens to click on your Google ad, and then they visit your site, and who knows what else they may be doing at that very moment? **(They may be at work, or doing some other activity online and just happened to stumble across your ad, etc, etc, etc!)**

Plus, they may not get enough out of the Etology-type sell-off pages upon their first visit – and the Net is one of those things where **"Mr. Fickle-Finger"** gets restless and decides to take off; and most likely forget your webpage altogether.

Just ask yourself how many webpages you've made a mental note to return to, and you've long since forgot exactly where and who they were, right?

But by using **option 2** above, you can capture their name and email and using AWeber: http://bit.ly/NMxDo you can send them both more educational emails letting them know more about what you are doing, and also send them announcements periodically with more offers to advertise on *this* or *that* webpage!

Using option 2 you can build a relationship with potential advertisers **(*Remember, all you usually need are just 6 to 15 advertisers for any one specific webpage to be completely offset from its Google AdWords campaign in order to eliminate YOUR costs, and to allow your main offer to ride for <u>FREE</u>! – and getting just 6-15 advertisers from 100's clicking on your ads at Google, and filling out your email form is a cinch!)** I sincerely hope you've gotten a most revealing lesson out of all this.

Where You Can Get the "Cash" Code

As I mentioned earlier there are a good number of online companies that provide this kind of "cash" code; and each is a little bit different from the others.

You will have to decide which one or ones fit the bill for your own interests. Although there are more than the ones below, these I've found to be the choicest and **BEST** ones to work with:

https://www.adbrite.com/mb/publisher_landing_page3.php

http://www.adengage.com/sellads.cfm

http://www.adjungle.com/publishers.html

http://www.adsbay.co.uk/

http://www.adspace-auctions.com/

https://www.adster.com/account/publisher_signup.php

http://bannergarage.com/Register.aspx?new=true

http://www.emptyspaces.eu/

https://www.text-link-ads.com/publisher_signup.php
http://www.clickagents.com/Publishers.shtml

http://itsyourad.com/

You can also find a huge number of other similar firms that will provide you their "cash" codes so that people pay you to advertise on your webpages simply by clicking here:

http://www.google.com/search?hl=en&safe=off&rlz=1T4GGIH_enUS264US265&q=%22sell+ads%22

Or by doing a specific Google search!

Regardless of which one(s) you use, the point is that you should definitely get your feet really wet doing this.

This system is fantastic; and after a brief while you'll find yourself learning the ropes and creating a brand new source of income!

Then, you will find yourself finding more and more ways to get more and more webpages up that "rinse & repeat" this system so that you find yourself earning unusually large amounts of money!

Resources you may need in order to implement the instructions in this ebook:

1. My Free Website Builder: http://business.blinkweb.com/

2. Free AdWords Learning Center:

http://adwords.google.com/support/aw/bin/static.py?hl=en&page=learningcenter.cs

3. Free Advertising Tips:

http://www.google.com/search?hl=en&safe=off&rls=GGIH%2CGGIH%3A2006-51%2CGGIH%3Aen&q=free+advertising+tips

I Have a Special Gift for My Readers

I appreciate my readers for without them I am just another author attempting to make a difference. If my book has made a favorable impression please leave me an honest review. Thank you in advance for you participation.

My readers and I have in common a passion for the written word as well as the desire to learn and grow from books.

My special offer to you is a massive ebook library that I have compiled over the years. It contains hundreds of fiction and non-fiction ebooks in Adobe Acrobat PDF format as well as the Greek classics and old literary classics too.

In fact, this library is so massive to completely download the entire library will require over 5 GBs open on your desktop.

Use the link below and scan all of the ebooks in the library. You can select the ebooks you want individually or download the entire library.

The link below does not expire after a given time period so you are free to return for more books rather than clog your desktop. And feel free to give the link to your friends who enjoy reading too.

I thank you for reading my book and hope if you are pleased that you will leave me an honest review so that I can improve my work and or write books that appeal to your interests.
Okay, here is the link…
http://tinyurl.com/special-readers-promo
PS: If you wish to reach me personally for any reason you may simply write to mailto:support@epubwealth.com.
I answer all of my emails so rest assured I will respond.

Meet the Author

Dr. Leland Benton is Director of Applied Web Info, a holding company for ePubWealth.com, a leading ePublisher company based in Utah. With over 21,000 resellers in over 22-countries, ePubWealth.com is a leader in ePublishing, book promotion, and ebook marketing.

As the creator and author of "The ePubWealth Program," Leland teaches up-and-coming authors the ins-and-outs of today's ePublishing world. He has assisted hundreds of authors make it big in the ePublishing world.

Leland also created a series of external book promotion programs and teaches authors how to promote their books using external marketing sources.

Leland is also the Managing Director of Applied Mind Sciences, the company's mind research unit and Chief Forensics Investigator for the company's ForensicsNation unit. He is active in privacy rights through the company's PrivacyNations unit and is an expert in survival planning and disaster relief through the company's SurvivalNations unit.

Leland resides in Southern Utah.

Visit some of his websites
http://www.AddMeInNow.com
http://www.AppliedMindSciences.com
http://www.BookbuilderPLUS.com
http://www.BookJumping.com

http://www.EmailNations.com
http://www.EmbarrassingProblemsFix.com
http://www.ePubWealth.com
http://www.ForensicsNation.com
http://www.ForensicsNationStore.com
http://www.FreebiesNation.com
http://www.HealthFitnessWellnessNation.com
http://www.Neternatives.com
http://www.PrivacyNations.com
http://www.RetireWithoutMoney.org
http://www.SurvivalNations.com
http://www.TheBentonKitchen.com
http://www.Theolegions.org
http://www.VideoBookbuilder.com

Some Other Books You May Enjoy From ePubWealth.com, LLC Library Catalog

EPW Library Catalog Online
http://www.epubwealth.com/wp-content/uploads/2013/07/Leland-benton-private-turbo.pdf

EPW Library Catalog Download
http://www.filefactory.com/f/562ef3ea1a054f0a

www.ingramcontent.com/pod-product-compliance
Lightning Source LLC
Chambersburg PA
CBHW051827170526
45167CB00005B/2187